Conversations About Relationships

Exploring Ideas From Change Your Life Radio

Lucinda Curran

BUILDING
VITALITY

National Library of Australia Cataloguing-in-Publication entry
Author: Curran, Lucinda,
Title: *Conversations About Relationships: Exploring Ideas
From Change Your Life Radio* / Lucinda Curran

ISBN-13: 978-1497362345
ISBN-10: 1497362342

Series: *Conversations About*

Subjects:
        Interpersonal relations.
        Interpersonal communication.
        Social psychology.

Dewey Number: 158.2

Published by Building Vitality
        366 Rathdowne Street Carlton North VIC 3054 AUSTRALIA
        www.BuildingVitality.com.au

Photograph of Lucinda Curran by Steven Lloyd
        www.StevenLloydPhotography.com.au

Please leave your review of

**Conversations About Relationships:
Exploring Ideas From Change Your Life Radio**

At www.BooksByLucinda.com

Table of Contents

your notes

Introduction

In my fascination of understanding the human condition, this book explores ideas, concepts and beliefs about relationships. I really like this as a topic, because when you stop to think about it, you can't help but notice that we have relationships everywhere, with all sorts of people, animals and situations. Some relationships are beneficial, others are strained, but all give us the chance to grow.

So, I invited four esteemed guests onto Change Your Life Radio, so we could explore the theme of relationships in different ways.

Relationships are about the ways that we interact in the world. It may be with people, our pets, and even inanimate objects or concepts.

Relationships are complex and varied. Relationships can change over time. Most importantly, relationships can create change. I love this last part. It is like there is so much potential bottled up in any relationship, and when the time is right, the potential comes to light. It is exciting, unknown and sometimes difficult.

So how do our relationships create change?

Because often those that we have in our lives mirror ourselves. They may validate us, may shine like us, or even hold us accountable for the more hidden parts of our natures.

There is a dance that plays out between people and everything in their lives. It is in this dance where the potential lies. What is the next step? Who is leading? What happens when the music peaks?

I love the dynamic nature of relationships, and that every interaction is unique – that you can't assume someone will be exactly the same as when you last saw them, that your thoughts and beliefs have not shifted. It is unpredictable – it is alive. It is life.

So, in the following pages, I have taken ideas explored with my guests and stretched them, dug deeper, or twisted them somewhat. My aim is to make them accessible to anyone who is interested.

So, please, read on and enjoy!

Learning From Your
Greatest Spiritual Teachers

Guest: Karen Palmer, author of *The Secret To Puppy Love*

Karen is known as the Queen of Kindness. Her work focuses on animals, children and the environment. This episode was crammed with information and insights across this spectrum, and we are only going to touch on a few here.

Listen to the episode at http://bit.ly/CYLRKaren

The Fabric Of Life

Karen:

> Relationships are one of the most important things that we have in the human experience. I really believe that our relationships can be so much more deep and meaningful when we realise how precious each moment is.

> We have amazing opportunities to weave in and out of each other's lives. There's a beautiful tapestry I think that's kind of woven with all of our experiences and I feel as if there is a beautiful pull that brings us all to

each other and the invisible thread that connects us all is the animals.

The life we have with our pets especially is so precious and we really have this unconditional love, that we can learn so much from the animals and from the other people in our lives too, but it is really easy to connect with the pure love essence of an animal or nature or a child. When we start to see how we can improve our relationship with a pet, we can start to see how we can improve all the relationships in our lives too.

I love the analogy of the threads and the way that everything is interconnected. I have always enjoyed thinking of "the fabric of life" and the different ways you can see this.

If you get your magnifying glass you can follow a thread through a cloth. Some weaves are simply over-one-under-one. Others are more complex, such as the jacquard weaves where the different coloured threads create the pattern. Then you have those magical fabrics that change colour depending on the angle you look at them.

Then you can think of the junctions, where the warp and weft threads meet – like when our lives intersect for however long they do...

But listening to Karen made me wonder, are we the gaps not the threads, with the other "forces" (particularly our animals) creating the connections and interconnections?

Whether the gaps or the threads, the fabric of life is rich, deep and splendorous as we choose it to be.

Our paths intersect with others. This may be fleetingly, maybe not. But they do intersect. Why?

Karen went on to say that, "Every person and animal in our life is a divine assignment and we have lessons to learn from each experience..." She recommended that in a conversation or interaction with anyone, that we look first to the similarities and then learn from the differences.

I like this idea of creating a common ground from which to explore further. It is fascinating the way that ideas, beliefs and patterns are shaped so differently for each of us.

Creating a common ground is like creating a safe space – one of love, acceptance and respect. Really, this should be the first step in any relationship. When we take the fear out of the unknown, and find the commonalities, is it a lot easier to make sense of the differences.

When we were talking, Karen used getting to know family members for her example. But the same can be applied across borders.

Imagine if we could see the similarities between us and all the other people in the world. Imagine if we saw this first and foremost... and that all interactions were based on respect, love and kindness. The world would be much more harmonious.

It sounds grandiose to create this as a goal – but if each one of us were to adopt this approach within our worlds, then we can start to see the flow on effect.

Imagine if your home life was filled with joy, laughter and love. You could leave the house with a heart full of happiness. Each encounter you have would be pleasant and harmonious, and if there is any tension, it can be soothed easily as you aren't caught up in anguish and angst.

I almost feel like breaking into John Lennon's "Imagine" – I always get tingles from that song.

But, can you see that by each and every person taking a stance, being proactive in creating harmony, greeting everyone with acceptance and not judgment that this is actually achievable?

It is when there is fear, judgments and mistrust that problems arise. This goes for interpersonal relationships, community relationships and even international ones. For that matter, it can even be intergalactic.

I say this, because of the alien hype that started in 50 years ago. There was fear – aliens were going to come and take over our planet. When the aliens do come they will be greeted with guns so that we can obliterate them before they obliterate us. But, what if they were coming in peace? What if there was no hostility on their part. What a wasted opportunity for humanity to grow and develop because of insecurity, paranoia and arrogance. Arrogance? I think so. This arrogance stems from our species' superiority complex - the belief that humans are superior to everything else.

So how much of this plays out in our everyday lives? Where are we being insecure, paranoid and arrogant? What can we learn from this in order to move on?

If we can see the beauty in everything, accept that everything in life really does come from a loving place, and that we can take responsibility for our lives, we really can change the world.

If we can accept what Karen said, that each life we encounters is on a divine assignment then things can really take a wonderful turn.

Look for those lessons, nurture those relationships and nourish the lives that are in ours.

This can be the key that turns your life around.

One thing I have always done is thanked my dogs for the lessons that they have taught me, the things I have learned because of them, and the ways that my life is better because they have been a part of it. I have done that as they have neared their time of passing. I wonder, as I sit with my Puppy, who is 14½, who is surviving all the health hurdles that are coming his way, isn't this something we should do more often? What would happen if we thanked our pets, our families, and our friends for these things on a regular basis? If we even stopped on a regular basis and just noticed all of these things, what would our lives be like then?

I really believe that humans have the power of language and that is something we can use to improve the human condition. We can express our gratitude, we can say thank you for the lessons, we can explain how our lives are enriched because of those in it – so why don't we?

I feel like we should have a monthly international "Gratitude Day" where we can express our thanks for those intangible things that happen in our lives because of the richness that others bring to it.

What do you think?

your notes

Living Fearlessly

One of the concepts that Karen talked about was recognizing that "the light inside cannot be extinguished." She was talking about the concept that what makes us who we are – the unique something inside us – the soul – our essence.

This is a concept that I mentioned in *Conversations About The Self* – using my language for the same idea, "life is an energy and energy cannot be destroyed."

You lose the fears associated with the limitations of our time on this planet when you recognise that your uniqueness is something eternal.

When you lose these fears, you are able to more fully explore and live out what you are meant to be doing.

I am lucky, because as a small child, I knew that I was here to make the world a better place. I had no idea how, but at least I was very strongly aware of that. I was the primary school political activist, sending petitions to the government as an eight year old, fighting for animal rights, trying to educate my community about keeping my local park clean, and desperately trying to stop people from smoking – at least in my presence. As I grew older, I decided that to change the world, I would become a teacher. At the same time, I studied politics and women's studies and was very politically active. Realising that our political system was too entrenched for me to crack on my own, I retreated. After some time in hibernation, I embarked on a new direction, which lead me to where I am now. I now feel that I am finally on the right path to making the world a better place.

But what if you have no idea of what you are here to do?

I'm going to be contrary and say that you do know, you just can't remember!

What I suggest you do, is work on your own spirituality – make time in your life to be quiet, to reflect, to ask questions. Think about what you like, don't like and what feels right. Develop your "gut instinct" and listen to it.

This last point is really important. I have had many conversations with people that have relied on others to tell them what they are here for, and it hasn't felt right... My suspicion is that the other person was projecting and telling them what their own purpose was.

If you haven't worked on your "gut instinct" or intuition before, this is a good thing to work with early on. What it is about is tapping into your innate knowingness of what is right for you.

Scruffy, My Teacher

I am going to share a story about my first Skye terrier, Scruffy.

One of the biggest lessons he wanted me to learn was to trust my instincts (or my gut, my intuition, my higher self). I am sure he had tried in the first little while of our lives together, but there was an incident that was so blindingly obvious – and one that I nearly didn't learn from... and that is the one I am going to share.

Scruffy was nearly 2 years old. We lived in the Blue Mountains with Monstar (an Australian Silky terrier). Where we lived was very much a part of the national park, and quite "wild" – which I loved. There were loads of bush rats, and recently some had taken up residence inside my roof. This was a problem on many levels, particularly as the fire brigade had to be called one night because a rat had chewed through the electrical wires and draped himself over them – and nearly caused a fire.

Wanting to prevent further hazards, and having tried everything else first, I resorted to calling a pest controller. He'd come and placed poison in my roof. Yet several weeks later, the rats were still there.

On his return visit, he brought in his bucket of green poisoned pellets and placed them on the ground. I hesitated – and was going to ask him about covering it or putting it up on the table, but before I had the chance he and Monstar had gone inside – and Monstar being Monstar, needed to be held to prevent him climbing the ladder and exploring the roof, the rats and the poison.

When we went back outside to get the poison, Scruffy had knocked the bucket over and was looking very guilty. Scruffy *never* did anything wrong, so having knocked the bucket this was enough to explain his guilty posture.

But, I was worried he had eaten it. I checked his gums and mouth and saw no signs of the green. My instinct was to take him to the vet – but the whole time, the pest controller was talking and talking… He was telling me things about how the poison contained a taste deterrent, that Scruffy would have needed to eat a bucket of the stuff for it to have any affect… blah… blah… blah. I listened to him – he was the expert – it was his poison, he knew how to use it.

So, we didn't go to the vet. And, like every other Monday, I travelled 100 kilometres to Sydney, visit my parents, attend my class at university, before coming home late that night.

The next morning, we started our walk, and Scruffy defecated. It was solid green – the exact same colour as the poison. It was an enormous poo – and it was only poison. He *had* eaten a whole lot of it.

I raced him off to the vet. They didn't seem to believe me. They kept him for observation. He didn't exhibit any of the classic signs of this type of poisoning (which was bleeding).

For days, they seemed dismissive of the whole idea as they had not seen the poo and Scruffy was not visibly bleeding.

On Thursday, I took him for a run in the park. That night he coughed up so much blood that the vets finally took notice of what I had said. It was only then that the decided to test his blood, and found that it was clotting ten times too slowly. This meant, like the rats, he was slowly bleeding to death.

He had an urgent blood transfusion, thanks to an anonymous big black dog that kindly donated to save his live. The vets were sure that he would not make it. I contacted everyone I knew and everyone that they knew for help. Every two hours I gave him his homeopathic remedy and herbs. All the healers in the Blue Mountains were doing their bit... One reiki practitioner called me and told me that she had expected to connect with a dying dog, but instead she found a dog that was surrounded by "rainbows of love and support" (they were her words from nearly 15 years ago – I still remember them – and they still bring tears to my eyes). The next few nights, Monstar took himself off to bed and I lay with Scruffy on the floor, waking every two hours to give him the next dose. Holding him close, wishing for him to survive.

Miraculously, he did.

My sweet boy nearly lost his life in this attempt to teach me to trust my own judgment, my instincts and my intuition. It took that momentous event for me to finally "get" it.

Scruffy lived until he was almost 11 years old. Sadly, it was cancer that took him – and I believe that this was from the poisoning.

So, the moral to this story is, learn the lessons when we are being taught them more subtly, because when we don't, the lessons get more and more confronting and the consequences can be more dire. Be present, be watchful and really tune into those around you. Each and every life we meet offers lessons for us to learn.

Trust your instincts – listen to yourself – go by whether things feel right, or not. Get that without learning it the way I did.

What you will notice is that you are 100% right about everything.

I used to notice my impressions of people – and when they were good, I would go with it, and when there was something not so good, I would give them the benefit of the doubt. "It's only fair," I would tell myself. Well, it wasn't fair to me. I gave them the benefit of the doubt and time and time again, they would prove to me what my first impression was correct 100% of the time.

So, learn to trust your inner knowing.

When you do, as you explore the world – trying to work out your path, you will have your bearings in tact. You will be able to follow the signs more easily and traverse a smoother road.

As you work on developing this, start exploring what you are drawn to and what you are repelled by. The reason to explore both is that even if you aren't totally clear yet on what you are here for, you may get clearer on what you are not here for. The process of elimination comes in handy for this!

Spend some time wandering and pondering – and develop your own radar for what is right for you. Nobody can be clearer than you on this – and this is an empowering skill to develop.

your notes

The Roadmap to
Caregiving Without Regret

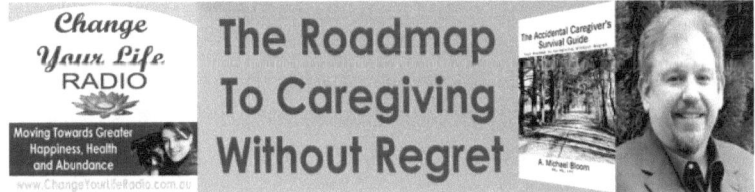

Guest: A. Michael Bloom, author of *The Accidental Caregiver: Your Roadmap To Caregiving Without Regret*

Michael fell into the role of being a caregiver when both of his parents needed assistance. It was not planned, but came about because of the change to his father's health. It is this sudden stepping into the role that is termed being an "accidental caregiver." It is a situation whereby a person is thrown in the deep end – often completely without warning.

You can listen to the episode here at
http://bit.ly/CYLRMichael

Living Without Regret

Michael

Caregivers tend to have potentially two major regrets that can happen during their journey of care.

One is that a lot of caregivers, and this is the one that I did was that I actually left my full-time professional career and devoted myself to caring for my parents.

In the initial months, or actually in the initial year that I was in that role I tried to be superman. Like many caregivers you try to do it all yourself.

So I stepped away from things I was doing in my professional and personal life to dedicate myself fully to my parents... and you never get that time back. So if caregivers do this over weeks, months or years, you can build up regrets and resentment for the care-giving role because you give up things that you have done before.

The other thing that tends to happen, that caregivers face regret with is that because you are walking hand-in-hand with your loved one through some of the most stressful situations that you will ever know. These truly are life-and-death situations. It's not just being upset because your favourite TV show was pre-empted one night or some other thing and you missed your TV show, or you lost a material item. Those are reasons to potentially get a little stressed, but when you are caring for loved ones who are going through really challenging and heart-wrenching, painful medical treatments, unknowing where the path of the illness or disease will take you it's a very stressful journey.

Because you and your loved one are so super-stressed, sometimes you say or do things that maybe you can regret later because you're so stressed.

One of the biggest things that I like to share with folks is just to acknowledge your humanness. Acknowledge and validate yourself for being in that caregiving role... you are human and sometimes you will say something that maybe you wish you hadn't said... so apologise for it.

Regret is to feel sorrow, sadness or disappointment about

something that occurred. On a personal level, regret eats away at us later with the "what ifs" and the "if onlys." Regret can be very damaging – and can play a massive role in our lives – if we let it. Regret can be a major part of the baggage that we lug with us through our lives.

In my mind, regret is an avoidable emotion. Wouldn't our passage through life be a whole lot easier if we didn't have to lug with us so many tales of pain?

I think Michael really hit the nail on the head when he pointed out that we should acknowledge humanness.

When we step down off our pedestals of being "super-people," we can put aside the ego, tuck the chest back in and be more humble. Humility is a trait that we can all incorporate into our lives.

Let's look at an example.

Pete was having a bad day.

It started as soon as he got up – he tripped over his laptop that he'd been working on before going to sleep, bumped into the doorframe and collected a nice bruise on his forehead. He made himself his morning jump-starter and found that there was no milk. No milk meant no coffee. No coffee meant no patience. His blood began to boil. Off to the shower, only to find that there was no hot water either! Pete shivered his way through his bathing before getting dressed and heading out the door.

His bus was late. It was crowded. The guy next to him clearly was on his way home from his "a big night out" – and he smelt like it! The driver missed his stop.

Pete sprinted to work – only just making it into the meeting. He sank into a chair, reached for the coffee in front of him and then remembered he'd left his notes on his desk. It was too late to dash out to get them.

The meeting started. The floor was his. He knew his stuff, but he was flustered. Without his notes, he was sure to forget something. This was the deal breaker, and he could feel the room swallowing him up.

He talked – it felt like he was underwater. He moved through his presentation. He finished – just. A colleague asked him a question. Pete gulped. He could feel everyone's eyes on him, and the boss' eyes boring into his skull.

The pressure built. His face reddened. He could hardly breathe.

Then he snapped.

He verbally let loose on his colleague.

He stammered. He stopped. He knew he was out of line.

He knew he had gone too far.

Pete lost control. He said things in anger – and his anger wasn't anything to do with the colleague who had asked him a simple question. It had nothing to do with anything other than a set of circumstances that played out.

Pete is human – he didn't handle the stressors at all well. But he is human.

So, what should he do?

Should he keep lamenting about what a horrible day he was having? Should he beat his chest and maintain that people shouldn't ask dumb questions? Or should he apologise?

His behaviour is clearly regrettable – but he *can* take action. Apart from better organisation skills, and perhaps even stress management, he can apologise for his behaviour.

Apologising takes courage. You have to be "big" enough to step up to the table and admit that you were wrong. You need to genuinely say that you are sorry. You also have to deal with the consequences of your actions – and hear what the other person has to say.

I believe that the best apologies are heart-felt ones. Receiving an empty apology is worse than not getting one at all. You've experienced those? When someone says, "I'm sorry," and you know that they are only saying it because they think they should. That there is nothing that they are sorry for – they are just saying it to make you happy.

Reaching a point where you can apologise from the heart can sometimes take time. In Pete's situation, he needed to calm down first. In other situations, it can be immediate, or it can take longer. I believe it is better to have a genuine one, than a rushed empty one.

Pete example is pretty extreme.

There are plenty of daily occurrences that you might want to apologise for – and if you are even slightly worried about having done something to wrong another, it is better to apologise than not.

It is amazing how mountains grow in your head – from the tiniest of mounds. From what I have experienced and observed, we judge how "big" the situation was based on the level of emotions that we were experiencing at the time.

I have had situations where I have been under a lot of stress and felt like I had been "short" with people. Oft times, I would apologise – having been painfully aware of how intense my stress was, and had the person I was apologising to being almost unaware of what I was referring to.

I have to say, if I hadn't have apologised, it would have bothered me. It would have stewed away in the background, and I would have felt like I had hurt them unintentionally... I need to resolve these sorts of things.

When I was about twenty years old I still had my tendency to apologise for everything – stuff that I wasn't sorry for and had nothing to do with me. That sounds really weird, but it is a common enough trait.

Now, in my defense, this was nowhere near what the character Willy does, in the Anthony Browne's picture storybook *Willy The Wimp*.

Willy apologised for everything – he even to the pole that he bumps into. (If you haven't seen this book, do read it – Anthony Browne is an amazing author and illustrator, and there are so many layers in his stories – which I think are for adults just as much as they are for children.)

Let me share an example.

A friend and I had gone out to dinner. She and I both started to order at the same time. I said, "I am sorry."

Silly example, but it was an occasion just like this when a stranger commented on what had happened. Her comment was, "I don't say sorry, because I don't do anything I regret."

I love these random interactions – because this is often where the gems of life are presented to you.

"Wow! So, you never say, 'sorry'?"

"Never."

Naturally, that got me thinking.

How do you live a life that you never have to say "sorry?"

And, one day, the answer came.

You simply think about everything and make the best choice possible.

No doubt you've heard me raving on about "responding and reacting" – if you haven't, please refer back to *Conversations About The Self*.

But this was supercharging the concept. This was "respond"

on steroids.

This was all about doing your best in every situation.

The gem had grown into gold.

No one can ever do more than their best. Someone's best is just that.

> *Good, better, best.*
>
> *Never let it rest...*
>
> *Until the good is better*
>
> *And the better is best.*

So, if you always do your best, you can't have regrets.

"But..." I hear you ask. "But, what if it wasn't your best?"

Then I will ask, "Was it the best in that moment – given what you knew, how you felt and what was going on?"

The key here is to accept that hindsight will always shed a different light on things. Hindsight is a great one for creating regret that gnaws away at you.

So, be the master of your own mind – accept that if you had the current knowledge back then, you may have done things differently. But, given you did not know what you do know then, then you made the best choice at the time.

Do you see how liberating this is?

The steps are simple. When you are in a situation, follow this process:

   1. Pause – you need some distance from the situation to be clear-headed

   2. Reflect – what is going on?

   3. Either mentally or on a piece of paper, list our your choices...

   4. Identify the consequences for each.

5. Explore each one – and your reasons for choosing them. For instance, if you are leaning towards one more than another because you are so angry about what is happening, then you need to recognise this is your reason.

6. Make the best choice from your list.

That's it!

That is the key to living without regret.

Now, I do want to emphasise that even when you follow this system, it is possible to do things that need apologies. So, if or when that happens, step up to the table and say what you need to say.

The worst that can happen is you can clear the air on something that has been festering for all involved, and the best is that the other person had no idea of a problem!

Be brave and do your best!

Finding Time To Care For Yourself When You Are Busy Caring For Others

When your primary responsibility in life is the care of others, taking care of yourself is often quite difficult.

You may be in a caregiving role – looking after elderly parents, siblings or family, perhaps you are a parent, or nursing a sick pet. When you are caring for others who really need you, it can be very hard to prioritise your own self-care.

I could argue the obvious – it is times like this that it is <u>most</u> important to take good care of yourself. However, I understand that it is hard to make your own needs a priority, particularly when you are caring for someone who is ailing.

I have explored the concept of daily self-care in *Conversations About The Self*, so I won't elaborate here, what I will explore is finding a way to make time for you when you are in the role of caring for others.

The step that is most likely to be overlooked is maintaining regular contact with health professionals who are looking after you. Increasing the frequency of your appointments with them and being honest about your circumstances and feelings will allow them to assist you better. By holding information back from them, you are limiting the ways that they can assist you. This is a time when you also need a lot of support. You can't give support and care to those you are looking after when there is nothing left to give, or you are burnt out, or resentful.

I think journaling can also be a useful tool in this situation. The joy of this is that it is just you releasing your thoughts, feelings and emotions. It is a safe way to vent everything – a bit like the pressure release valve on a pressure cooker.

Another important step that you can take is to identify the things that make you happy - the things you enjoy doing.

Think of hobbies, interests and desires. Work out what is realistically achievable. It is unlikely that you can go bushwalking everyday, but you may be able to go fortnightly. Then organise some time out for yourself.

Clearly, if those you are caring for need 24-hour care, you will need to find someone to cover for you.

Michael suggested using the free online tool www.lotsahelpinghands.com that can be used to get support from your community or from others who are willing to help out.

We talked about creating lists of the daily, weekly, monthly and as-needed tasks and responsibilities. This is a great thing to do for numerous reasons.

Firstly, you can show it to others in your community who offer help. The list of tasks can allow them to identify what they would be willing to do to help. There is a lot of benefit to people selecting their own tasks.

Another benefit is that if you are taking some time out, you can hand the list over to whoever is filling in for you. This makes their life easier as they know what is required.

Also, if you have someone who is willing to do a regular task for you, you can take this regular break. Is there someone who can come by each Thursday morning with the groceries... and allow you to go the park and read a book?

Michael made the point that, "no one's going to perform at the level you do because nobody is you." So if you can hear that, you can accept that others can help in their own way, and this will free you up a little to take some care of yourself.

Being a caregiver is an enormous pair of boots to walk in. You hear, see and experience the joys, pains and thoughts of your loved one on a daily basis. Be kind to yourself, and allow yourself to have time out on a regular basis. It does not mean that you begrudge your role, you resent your loved one or anything else – it just means that you can accept that you are human, and that you need to replenish yourself too.

For everybody in the caregiving role, I offer you my respect – it is a mighty role you are fulfilling. Kudos to you!

your notes

Prayer Prescriptions That Heal

Guest: Kate Loving Shenk author of *The Prayer Prescription Series*

Kate has worked as a nurse for three decades, with most of her work being in women's health and paediatrics. Her approach to life and prayer is from a spiritual perspective and is her approach to death.

Listen to the episode here at http:/bit.ly/CYLRKate

Life Time

In our discussion on prayer and meditation, Kate shared her understanding of how the two work together as a conversation with God, Goddess, and Spirit, where prayer is where we are talking and meditation is where we are listening.

I asked Kate her perspective when people say that they don't have time to meditate.

> I believe that not having time is just an attitude. You can view time as being finite or infinite.

When you look at time as finite there aren't enough hours in the day, etcetera. Then you really do believe and you really get yourself into a box and it is easy to become overwhelmed, it is easy to become constricted, uptight and tense.

But when you look at life and time as being infinite... and that time doesn't even exist that you can be much more productive and get so much more accomplished with that attitude...

To have a daily practice of prayer and meditation automatically helps you change your perspective...

You find that lots of things just don't bother you like they do if you don't have a practice or if you let your practice lapse. Then all of a sudden things kind of crowd in on you, you're just not feeling fully dimensional, you're not feeling in tune with the great source...

I would say that a simple practice of meditation and prayer everyday will help that feeling of the infinite timeless perception that really is needed for a joyous life.

I find the concept of time fascinating because the way it feels depends so much on what is going on... For instance, you are sitting in a one-hour lecture that is incredibly boring. Every second feels weighted and the hour drags on and on, seemingly without end. Another time, you could be visiting your best friend, and all of a sudden, you realise three hours have passed.

They do say, "Time flies when you're having fun," but how?

How does it bend, stretch and retract? How is it so changeable?

Or is it?

If we step back to examine this, we know that time is a human construct. Based on the fact the sun rises and sets, and we gauge our days as passing by this phenomena, then we begin to see how, as humans, we have broken this down into chunks that we can "manage."

If we have 24 hours in a day, we can sleep for 8, work for 8 and have 8 left for everything else.

We have created pigeonholes for blocks of time that we measure externally with a clock.

But what is time?

What popped into my head was a children's story by Janet and Allan Ahlberg that appeared in their collection, *The Clothes Horse And Other Stories*. It's kind of a twisted set of stories exploring concepts that we use in our everyday language.

The particular tale is about "life savings." It is all about how a girl who started her life savings. From a youngster, she started putting away portions of her life. When she became quite old, she decided to spend her life savings.

Please bear with me, I haven't read this book in over a fifteen years, so I am not going to be accurate in my recollection, but you will get the gist of it from what I relay.

She had saved 20 minutes from when she was 4, 3 hours from when she was a teenager, half a day from primary school, and all sorts of different amounts at different ages. Then, as an elderly woman, went and spent them – so she played in the park, she ran around, she felt a little listless as a teenager, and so forth.

I read this book when it came out in 1992 as I was already a big fan of their work – I trained to be an early childhood teacher, and discovered their work at teachers college. Later I did my MA in Children's Literature. This will explain my references to children's books – they are so rich on every level. But I digress; when I first read this story, it really got me thinking about time and what it meant. I don't recall ever coming up with anything concrete, but it has always been an open-ended concept that I toy with when I get time (pun intended).

Is it possible to save these portions of our lives? Can we, in essence, bottle them for later use? Is there any reason why this is not possible?

As I say, I have never really answered these questions. And, as is often the case, one question creates many more.

Coming back to what Kate said about the infiniteness of time, she was not necessarily talking about making the most of time or managing it well – although these do lead to being productive.

My sense is that it is a lot more to do with the idea that there is no time limit... that our lives aren't over when we die, so that our time doesn't end at that point.

This throws my existential notions out the window, or at least suspends them, because we begin to move into an area that is not known and cannot be known. It is a little like the Dao – the Dao that can be spoken of is not the true Dao. So we are really discussing illusions of concepts that we cannot be certain of.

I have always been fascinated by Isabelle Allende's work, well in fact, much of the magic realism genre. If you are not familiar with her work, particularly her earlier work, the deceased and living members of the families that she wrote of were all present much of the time. They communicated and interacted in almost an unchanged way.

A few years prior to discovering her work, I had come up with the notion that, "life is an energy, thus it cannot be destroyed." Which would mean that when we die, our energy shifts in some way.

It still exists, but not in the way that it had. Allende's work seemed like a way it could make sense. It was as though the deceased were in another dimension that co-existed with the world of the living.

I have no way of knowing the truth of these ideas, I have my philosophers heart, so unanswered questions, "open" concepts, and ambiguous ideas do not cause me to feel disquieted.

Perhaps Allende's stories capture the truth?

If they do, then clearly we can still keep working on our life's purpose without having the physical form that we know now. If this is the case, then time can be without limit.

Pondering this, I have turned to the Daoist philosophy text, the *Dao De Jing* by Lao Tzu. The Dao is the Way, the path… Here, Lao Tzu seeks to define it.

> There was something undefined and complete, coming into existence before Heaven and Earth. How still it was and formless, standing alone, and undergoing no change, reaching everywhere and in no danger (of being exhausted)! It may be regarded as the Mother of all things.
>
> I do not know its name, and I give it the designation of the Tao (the Way or Course). Making an effort (further) to give it a name I call it The Great.
>
> Great, it passes on (in constant flow). Passing on, it becomes remote. Having become remote, it returns…
>
> (Chapter 25 from the *Dao De Jing*)

The Dao is seen as what existed before all else, and all stemmed from there. Much like in other faiths, where there was an entity or God that existed from which all else began.

So, in this chapter, there is discussion of the idea of this "energy" being in constant flow, and that this movement creates distance, which naturally results in its returning. It suggests to me the constant passage, the to-ing and fro-ing, the change that is inherent in all things. There is a constant movement, and interdependence of opposing states that there is oscillation between. Is this the flux of time, and for that matter of life?

Perhaps this adds more to the conversation... What are your thoughts?

Walking The Dog

Kate and I are both avid dog-lovers and we talked about the different ways to walk your dog. One thing that abhors me is the number of people that take their dog out while they go for a run. In these instances, the walk isn't for or about the dog. It is about the person getting their exercise, and dragging the dog along, too. A modern multi-tasking that defeats the beauty of the walk.

Walking your dog can be your meditation.

Walking with your dog, which is my preferred wording, is about taking him or her for their adventure. They need to sniff, mark territory, run, walk, dawdle and explore. Each tree is like a newspaper filled with the latest news. Each smell is a delight and a rich language. Each step is so sacred, as each is perceived as new, even if the path is familiar.

To walk with your dog is to experience their walk with them, at their pace, doing what they do.

My first dog, Monstar found joy in everything. His world-view meant that everything he encountered was a plaything. He had a knack of getting everyone to play with him. When he was 3 months old, we were walking in the park and many of the trees had lost their leaves. As he walked, the leaves crunched underfoot. He was surprised, paused, sniffed, listened... and took another step. Soon he realised what was causing the sound, and then the games began.

I remember Scruffy's first time at the beach. I had never noticed the loud roaring of the waves as much as I did that day with him.

Dear Puppy had to learn how to enjoy a walk. He had previously lived in an unhappy home for 6.5 years, and only left the home once, when he was taken to the rescue shelter. When he came to live with me, he did not seem to understand the purpose of a walk. It took years before he began to slow down, sniff and explore his environment.

Walking with your dog means you are present. Your mind isn't racing off in the distance, or lagging behind in the past. You are here and now, with your dog.

There is such a beauty in walking with them and learning to see the world their way. Personally, I have found this to be an incredible part of the bonding process. It helps you to relate better to them. It helps them feel safe and secure in exploring the world. It brings so much joy. I often catch myself laughing on walks.

Kate defined meditation as the time where we listen to Source, God, Goddess... It is the quiet time, the still time. It is where we are present, and open. Walking with your dog can create this state in an instant.

Being present and mindful – aware of every movement, sensation, and emotion. Being watchful and open to understanding. Being at one with your dog while you explore the world together.

This can be a part of your daily practice and it can help with the bond that is needed to learn lessons from each other, as Karen and I discussed.

In my mind, this daily routine of walking WITH your dog can be the simple key to shifting the focus in your life.

If you don't have a dog, try walking with the same sense of exploring the world for the first time. Notice the flowers, the trees, the sky, the smells, the sounds, and the feel of the world all around. Enjoy every step, every breath and every moment.

Try it.

Life After Divorce: 7 Steps To Recovery

Guest: Martin Salama, author of *Recovering From Divorce: 7 Steps To Recover Without Drama To Create A New Life*

Martin became a Divorce Recovery Coach as a result of his 24-year long marriage ended. He shared many tips, strategies and insights that are applicable not only to divorces, but also to any endings.

Listen to the episode here at http://bit.ly/CYLRMartin

How Do You Know When It's Over?

I asked Martin if the Orthodox Jewish faith accepted divorce. My concern was that there was the extra burden of the religious community not condoning the ending of a marriage that wasn't working – making the decision and process all the more difficult.

Here's what he said:

> It does accept divorce. It is written in the Old Testament all about divorce and the things that you have to do. But what happens is, especially in the Orthodox sect of the religion, is that the Rabbi's really try to discourage it [often] to the point of detriment to

the couple. I've heard so many stories where the wife will come to the Rabbi say, "He's abusive, he's this, he's that. I want out of this." And the Rabbis will tell the women, "No. It's important to stay married. It's so important to stay married, you have to stay married."

Of course, you want to do everything you can. But there are some times when it's just not a good fit. It could be the first

few years, or it could be twenty-five years later. Things happen.

I talk about this in my book. Love, in general, is not a feeling… it is a decision. It's a decision that you both have to make every single day of your life. When you get up in the morning you are making the decision that you are with the person and that you want to be with them.

If you're not making those decisions then it's never going to work.

So, how do you determine that something doesn't work anymore?

What I am going to explore is not, what I consider, the more obvious situations where there is physical or psychological abuse. If those situations were relevant, then I would make a blanket statement that things are never going to get better, and you are best off getting out before they get worse. Set up your support networks, find a shelter and leave – forever.

I wanted to explore the situations where it is unclear.

To me, what is fundamental in a relationship is love, trust, friendship and mutual respect. I also expect good communication and honesty.

For me, I would rather know the truth, even if it were painful, that to be lied to. I think the feelings of unease when there are lies are enough to make you feel like you are going mad, particularly when you ask if there is a problem and you get told categorically that there isn't.

So, working out when things are over can be tough.

I would suggest that when there is a heaviness in your heart, a sadness when you see the other person, an emptiness that has gone on for too long are all good signs to watch for.

How long is too long? Well, that is hard to measure in weeks, months or years. My answer to that would be if it has reached the point where you don't think it can ever get better.

All relationships have their ups and downs, but when the downs are unending, when there is no sense of hope, when your soul feel burdened by the relationship, it may be time.

Now, this applies to any relationship – friends, family, partners, colleagues, neighbour, whoever.

If there is no hope left, and you have exhausted all attempts, it may be time to call it a day.

What is important to each relationship will vary from person to person, I listed what was most important to me just before.

What matters most to you?

Have a good think about it. Have a good talk about it. Search your heart, your soul, your mind. Seek support from a psychologist. Talk to people trained in this area.

Have you tried therapy of some kind – couples, individual, family?

Is there any other avenue that you could explore to salvage your relationship?

If there is no way forward, this all needs to be brought out into the open.

I have always had a theory that it is harder on the "dumpee" than it is on the "dumper." I decided that this was the case because the person who ends the relationship is the person who has thought about it, rationalised it, perhaps sought professional help about it... They are prepared. If you are the "dumpee," you are the one that found out it was over, and you may not have seen it coming.

My advice is to always think about it from the "dumpee's" position. Start having those conversations, see what you can resolve.

I believe that often problems occur because people don't communicate. They have expectations of one another that are unclear and this sets the other person up for failure.

Just say your partner expected you to put toothpaste on both toothbrushes when you brushed your teeth first. Just say you had no idea. Every time you brushed your teeth and didn't put toothpaste on both brushes, the other person felt perturbed, upset or even resentful. Every time this happened, it built more and more resentment. The molehill becomes a mountain, which turns into a volcano that eventually erupts. The volcano didn't need to erupt, or exist in the first place. It all falls back to communication.

If you can have a relationship with others where you can clearly communicate with each other, be heard and respected, then potentially all problems can be resolved.

Having this sort of communication relies on self-awareness and honesty. You need to know who you are, how you feel and why you feel the way you do. You then need to communicate this in a way

that can be heard by the other person, without them feeling attacked.

A key way to communicate your needs is through "I-messages." I first heard about these in the 1970's, I am not sure how long they have been around...

Basically, you need to own your feelings and reasons.

Here are some examples:

"I feel sad and insecure when you go out late with your

friends. I would prefer it if you would occasionally invite me too."

"I get irate when you go off to work and I find you've left the dishes for me to do. I would prefer it if you would tell me that you ran out of time."

"I feel rejected every time you comment on how beautiful another woman is. I know it's irrational. I would like it if you would give me the same sort of praise."

Can you see how communicating your needs in this way helps the other person to understand what is going wrong for you, as well as what you would like to happen as a solution?

The three steps in creating an I-message are:

    1. I feel...

    2. When/because...

    3. I would like/prefer...

Give it a go – good communication, I believe, is the key.

Even if it is too late to save this relationship, it can help with the separation... and skill you up for all future relationships.

your notes

Always Speak Your Truth

Martin and I talked about reacting and responding, which is one of my favourite topics... I have written about it before.

For those who aren't aware of the difference, one way to understand it is that responding is the considered act that follows, whereas reacting is the knee-jerk one.

I like to illustrate concepts with stories, and in an article that I wrote, "Challenge Contains Change," I explained it in this way:

> *A small child licks an ice cream, enjoying the coolness, the colours and the taste of this delicious treat, when SPLAT! The ice cream lands on the hot ground.*
>
> *The child who reacts is the one who screams and cries.*
>
> *The child who responds is the one who is fascinated by their treat changing form, by the colours merging together and creating new ones, by the way the ice cream now runs along the ground following the slope and the cracks in the pavement.*
>
> *So when you are faced with a challenge, do you scream back at it? Or do you consider it, and find the golden lining?*

(You can listen to my narration of it here http://bit.ly/challengecontainschange)

This should give you a good idea as to what this is about.

In the same article, I also explained how life could feel at certain times – and I want to take you somewhere different afterwards.

There will be times when it feels like you are on a ship in rough seas. Where everything slides this way, then that. The movement of the boat is strong, it makes you feel sick and you become disoriented. Another wave crashes over the boat, drenching you from head to toe as you slip and slide to another edge. What do you do? How do you move forwards?
Where is forwards?

In times like these, it is often easiest to react. The blurt things out. To just do something, anything, in the hopes that everything will settle. It is in these tumultuous times that you can often lash out, say things in anger or be completely unreasonable.

To me, there is nothing worse than lashing out, saying things that are only partly true, or just saying things to be hurtful *just because you are hurting*.

It is a common thing for people to lash out and be hurtful when they are hurting. I am sure you can think of someone you know who has done this (and it may even be yourself).

If someone you know is behaving in this way, be the adult in the situation, and step out of it emotionally – don't hear, feel or think about the hurtful accusations. If you can, find a way to help them. Perhaps you could offer them a card for some counseling, the number for phone support, or a chance to sit down and have a proper talk (only do this if you feel you can handle it).

I encourage you to make time for yourself every single day – and particularly when the seas are rough. Spend time centering yourself, refocusing on what is most important and softening your way in the world.

When you know what is important, and you have had some time to steady yourself on the rocking ship, you will have some idea of how to move forwards.

If you don't make this time for yourself, it is possible that your eyes will be so blurred with salty water, your confusion so heightened and your feet so unsteady that you will head off in the wrong direction.

.So, even if it is just for five minutes a day – or the length of time it takes to sip your favourite cup of tea – spend this time on you. Be still. Be quiet. Ground, reorient, and refocus.

Honour your need for personal time and always speak your truth.

your notes

Bonus:
Discover How To Live On Higher Ground

Guest: Paul Lawrence Vann author of *Living On Higher Ground*

Paul is one of the kindest, most positive and inspiring people that I have ever had the pleasure of meeting. He was a guest on my show when we discussed "Wealth," but so many of his concepts relate to relationships. I wanted to share one of these with you – Paul lives and breathes this one, and I would love more people to do so, as well.

If you would like to hear the episode, you can listen in here at http://bit.ly/CYLRPaul

Legacy of Friendship

Paul was explaining some of the concepts included in his motivational and inspirational book...

Paul:

> "Building A Legacy Of Friendship Wherever You Go"

> This is one of the most important aspects both in personal and professional life because life really is about relationships. It's about building professional

relationships whether it is with colleagues, co-workers, as employers... And in our personal lives with our family, with our friends, with our colleagues.

So I think it is very important that people who read this book [*Living On Higher Ground*] would also glean that type of information in terms of how to go about opening up.

Everyone is not what you would call an extroverted person a lot of people are introverted persons, like I was at a very young age. So we have to have ways to overcome that and go out there and have these great relationships.

By Paul's example, being polite, respectful and positive are the most fundamental aspects to this.

Politeness, many today see as antiquated, but it is not. More than ever, to take a moment to offer some kindness via a polite act or word is a very powerful way to connect with people.

Have you had a complete stranger offer you their seat when you really needed it? Perhaps someone helped you to cross over the road? Maybe even a stranger smiled and said, "Good morning," to you. Doesn't it make you so happy?

All of these are acts of politeness. They are well-intentioned acts that demonstrate your generosity of spirit, your kindness and the fact that you are willing to take a moment and "extend a hand" to someone else.

Being respectful of another is about being non-judgmental towards them. It doesn't matter whether you vote for the same political party, you share the same religious beliefs, or you have the same eye colour – every person is treated with respect.

Earlier, I explored Karen's idea of finding the common ground before looking to the differences. This can be the foundation of respect. To respect someone is to hold them in high regard. It does not mean that you idolise them, but that you accept them for who they are.

For me, I have always sought to understand others and to be understood. It does not matter if we maintain our differing opinions, but to have shared a common understanding is crucial.

You may not respect everything about a person, you may live your life very differently, but it is important to find something you can respect in all the people you deal with.

Many years ago, I was struggling with some of my colleagues. At this time, someone offered this to me, and I now hold it as a truth. "You don't have to like your colleagues, but you need to get on with them."

I think this applies to all interactions with others – you don't have to like them, in that you want to spend time with them out of work (or wherever) but if they are in your life, you need to get on with them.

This led me to finding something I liked in everyone. If I could like something, I could respect it. If I could respect someone, it was a whole lot easier for me to get on with them.

Being positive is the third part of leaving a legacy of friendship.

Imagine you are on social media and you have a "friend" who continually drones on about all the miseries in life, how they are sick, how it's cloudy today, how it is sunny today, that they didn't like their meal, that everything is dark, murky and heavy.

In contrast, you have another "friend" who wishes you well, greets everyone, replies in an uplifting way, sees the golden lining in everything.

Which one leaves you feeling like you want to read more? This is the same as face-to-face.

We have all known (or been) that person that always has

troubles for friends to sort out, that launches into the dramas on the assumption that you've been waiting with baited breath for the next dire installment, or continually had something to whine about.

Well, how about switching it?

How about finding the good in every situation, celebrating the successes of those around you, offering encouraging words, kindness, support – even love – to those in your life?

Imagine (yep – John Lennon again) if everyone did this...

I encourage you to take a piece of paper, draw up three columns and give them the headings "polite," "respect" and "positive." Next, list out eight things that you can do under each of those headings.

Now, I **challenge** you to do one a day for the next month.

Watch the difference it makes in your life. Encourage others to do the same.

Go forth and make the world a better place.

With love and respect

Lucinda

Have You Enjoyed This Book?

I would really appreciate it if you would leave a review
on Amazon for me.

Visit www.BooksByLucinda.com to review
Conversations About Relationships:
Exploring Ideas From Change Your Life Radio

Resources

All books referred to in this book are available on Amazon. I also
have them in my online bookstore, which you can find at
http://CYLbook-store

There is further information about programs, courses and more just
a few pages on.

your notes

Acknowledgements

I want to take this opportunity to say a special thank you to my mother, Doreen Curran. All my life, she has showed me kindness, understanding and has always encouraged my in everything that I do. She has shown me the importance of approaching those in our lives with love and acceptance for who they are.

At 85, she is always the first person to read any of my work. Without her nod of approval, things don't make it out to you...

Both of my parents, unwittingly, gave their children a great gift – love, support and encouragement in every endeavour, whether or not they personally agreed or not. These behaviours were unconditional, and I know that if they were not like this, it would be a lot harder for me to be true to myself at a soul level, as I am not one that can be neatly placed in a box.

With these two people as my role models, it has put me in good stead to go out into the world and approach relationships with respect, love and acceptance. I thank them both for this.

This book is based on ideas that began during my conversations with my guests on Change Your Life Radio. So, I would like to formally thank them for sharing their wisdom, insights and expertise – and keeping my mind active with thoughts, ideas and ponderings. Thank you to Karen Palmer, A. Michael Bloom, Kate Loving Shenk, Martin Salama and Paul Lawrence Vann.

I also want to thank our mutual mentor, D'vorah Lansky for bringing us all together.

your notes

Dedications

To my community,
my dear ones
and YOU.

I hope that this book will bring you
ideas, insights and incentives to
make your life even better.

♥

Lucinda Curran

Interested In Meditation?

Claim your FREE guide:
The Simple Path To Meditation

From www.ChangeYourLifeRadio.com.au

Change Your Life Radio

Change Your Life Radio is a weekly event and centres around a monthly focus.

You can listen in from anywhere in the world – and you don't even have to listen in live because the show is recorded.

www.blogtalkradio.com/lucindacurran

About The Author

Healthy Life and Safe Living Consultant Lucinda Curran integrates Chinese medicine and Building Biology to provide truly holistic healthcare. Lucinda works with people who are keen to make changes towards achieving their optimal health.

Driven by passion and motivated by personal experience, Lucinda endeavours to help people make informed choices, provide viable solutions and make the world safer for all who dwell here.

She hosts the weekly **Change Your Life Radio show**, has authored books that focus more on the internal landscape of thoughts and beliefs, and is available for interviews, workshops and talks.

She is determined to bring a range of perspectives to her listeners and readers, primarily because there is no such thing as a one-size-fits-all. The smorgasbord of life exists for this reason - we all need different things at different times.

She lives in Melbourne, Australia with her Skye terrier.

You can listen to all of her radio shows at http://bit.ly/CYL-Radio

Programs

From ChangeYourLifeRadio.com.au:

Change Your Life: 50 Daily Meditation-Affirmations That Anyone Can Do (2013) this easy-to-use workbook teaches a simple meditation routine, includes 50 daily meditation affirmations and free access to a companion program.

Conversations About The Self: Exploring Ideas From Change Your Life Radio (2014) is a whimsical journey through the psyche based on ideas stimulated by conversations with my guests on Change Your Life Radio.

Conversations About Hidden Hazards In The Home: Exploring Ideas From Change Your Life Radio (forthcoming in 2014) this book explores safer options for many hidden hazards in the home. Be empowered through insights.

Starting Out Program is designed to help you to take the reins of your life and steer it in the direction that you want it to go in. This is an audio program.

5 Steps to Freedom Coaching Program is a one-on-one coaching program to help you achieve the freedom to live the life of your dreams. You set the pace.

From EcoHealthSolutions.com.au:

Living With Environmental Sensitivities is a free eCourse to help those suffering from environmental sensitivities manage it better.

Environmental Sensitivities Bootcamp an in-depth, motivating and life-changing bootcamp for anyone who has environmental sensitivities, especially those new to it.

Healthy Life Consultations and Coaching offers you insight into what might be impacting on your health from a Building Biology perspective.

Books By Lucinda Curran

The following are snippets from Lucinda's first two books.

If you like them, you can get your copies at
www.BooksByLucinda.com

From "Change Your Life: 50 Daily Meditation-Affirmations That Anyone Can Do"

FOCUS STATEMENT

Shine and succeed.

ADDITIONAL MEANING

Within your heart is your Light of Life. It is your Light. It is unique, precious and very beautiful. When you shine, truly shine, you give others permission to shine brightly, too. This is one of the greatest gifts that you can give to yourself, your dear ones and the planet. To shine allows us to succeed – for when we are living from our hearts, the path to success becomes smooth and easy to traverse.

ACTION STEP

Connect with your heart, and let it shine through your eyes.

~ ♥ ~

FOCUS STATEMENT

Leap into life.

ADDITIONAL MEANING

Clinging to the wall because you are frightened of shining is not living to your full potential. Instead, go out into the world from a place of love. Embrace every opportunity. Treasure every joy. Turn every hardship into a chance to grow.

ACTION STEP

What is stopping you from fulfilling your grandest dreams? What can you let go of? Write down what you are willing to release.

~ ❤ ~

FOCUS STATEMENT

The only thing you can do about the future
is to make the present as wonderful as possible.

ADDITIONAL MEANING

The present is a reflection of your old thoughts, feelings and beliefs. Thus, your present thoughts, feelings and beliefs shape your future. Focus your energy onto the positives – dream grandly, imagine the greatest, happiest and healthiest life for you.

ACTION STEP

What would your perfect life be like? How does it look, feel, and sound? Imagine and then record your ideal home, relationships, work and life.

~ ❤ ~

From "Conversations About The Self: Exploring Ideas From Change Your Life Radio"

Quiet Time is tough – and part of it is about challenging your current situation to reacquaint you with your innate direction that you may have become sidetracked from.

As Gail and I discussed, getting into a state of discomfort is a positive thing. Getting uncomfortable shows that you are going deep – and that is where change needs to take place.

If you are not uncomfortable, I would suggest that you are not in the right place. Thus, any changes you make are likely to be superficial.

Gail and I talked about change as being like getting into a body of water and having to let go of the edge to swim out over to the other side. As a swimmer, you can expect to get wet, know that you will be swimming… but you cannot see the other side.

If you are not a strong swimmer, letting go of the side can be extremely scary.

It is about stepping into the vortex of the unknown and having faith or trust that everything is going to work out.

This is the next step. It is about taking a leap of faith.

This is the part that, according to Gail, I am unusual. I love change. I wholeheartedly embrace it. For me, throwing everything up into the air to allow it to land wherever it does is fantastically exhilarating.

I love the feeling of wiping the slate clean. Of starting again; altering my path, my direction; stepping out and into my renewed self. I love the feeling of having no idea what is coming. But I love all of that because I **KNOW** that everything always works out for the best.

No matter what, I can look back at anything in my life – and no matter how painful, how torturous, how agonising it was at the time, it ALWAYS worked out for the best.

Often, it takes hindsight and time to see this.

Everything in life always works out for the best.

This is the outlook – well, more of a core belief – that gets me through. It is what I called my Rainbow-Coloured Glasses because Rose-Coloured Glasses just don't even come close.

So this next step, it is about trusting.

Have faith. Know that things work out for the best.

The final step is being courageous. Courage is the trait that I admire most. Courage is about following your heart, your dreams your beliefs; is about setting off on your own path – the one that is right for you; and courage is about not worrying about how others perceive you, what they think of you or potential criticism. If you get stuck here, you will be frozen for a long time.

People in our society have been conditioned to follow the norm, toe the line, and be like everyone else.

But to shine, you need to follow your heart, throw the line out to whoever wants to catch it, and to be YOU.

If you stop to worry about what others think or say or criticise, then you need to remind yourself that you are following your own path.

Be prepared: people who do this are judged. Why? Because when you do what you need to do, you are most likely breaking the mould of what is "normal." People who do not like this are threatened by it in some way. The biggest threat that I see is that you are making them look at their own lives. You are giving them reason to get out of their comfort zone... and we both know that this is not an easy process.

But, we both know, that it is a worthwhile process.

Also, the judgments of others are not always negative. Often people are inspired, motivated or excited by those that are true to themselves.

I encourage you to be bold – create some Quiet Time – ask questions, delve deeply and confront your "inners" – work out what you want to do – and be courageous.

And know in your heart that not only does everything work out for the best, but that you are inspiring others to do the same – to find their own path.

Finding your path, doing what you are here to do, and being true to your calling brings the utmost joy.

I know you can do it. Be brave. Leap into life.

your notes

Articles by Lucinda Curran

Lucinda took *Change Your Life: 50 Daily Meditation Affirmations That Anyone Can Do* and *Conversations About The Self: Exploring Ideas From Change Your Life Radio* on a virtual book tour in early 2014.

What's a "virtual" book tour? This is where Lucinda travelled through cyberspace to visit different communities around the globe. Her lovely hosts either interviewed her on radio or television, or published an article that she wrote.

To see her postcards and access the full tour, visit
http://bit.ly/myvbtpostcards

What follows are two articles that she wrote as part of the tour.

After that are some others from her blog – which you can read at www.EcoHealthSolutions.com.au

your notes

Life As A Student: 5 Steps to Maintaining a Healthy Balance

Being a student is such an exciting time – the buzz of learning new information, making new friends and discovering more about yourself all make it memorable.

Yet, there is the pressure, the timetables and the deadlines... Making it tough to maintain a healthy life balance.

So, before the Semester gets going, it is important to do some planning so that you not only meet your deadlines, but that you do so with ease, and ensure that you are taking care of your wellbeing.

I love studying, and at any given moment, I am always studying something. What I am going to share with you is the method that got me through one of the heaviest study period of my life. At one stage, I had 23 contact hours per week (classes and lectures) and well over 30 assessments per semester – and that went on for 5 years!

Here are my 5 steps to maintaining a healthy balance.

5. Creating Goals

I always recommend having a clear picture of what it is all about.

- Why are you studying?
- What will your life be like once you have completed this qualification?
- What will your work life be like?

Take some time to sit with these questions and really "get to know" your answers. Then, on a piece of paper, either draw or write down your answers.

These images and ideas are something that you will want to draw on when the pressure mounts (like during exam time). Having your goal clearly in your mind will give you the incentive, passion and motivation to get through.

4. Self Care

Taking care of yourself is vital. Student life is a lot about what I call the input-output cycle.

You go to lectures and tutorials and soak up information, you read your texts and other work, and you think, converse and play with new concepts. Then you write assignments, essays and exams. There are a lot of demands on a student.

From a Chinese medicine perspective, studying can weaken the digestive organs as well as create stagnation. So, from this point of view, I recommend maintaining a good diet of foods that are seasonal and easy to digest (soups, stews and casseroles are great student food as they are easy to prepare and can be eaten over several days). I also recommend exercise to help maintain your body – anything from walking to cycling, kick boxing to tai chi. Exercise will also help you to reduce your stress levels.

Other than that, make a list of the things that YOU enjoy – that you find nourishing and nurturing.

3. Assessing Your Semester

Once you start each of your subjects, you will have an insight into how much time you will need to spend on each subject, what your assessments are and when they occur.

You will also know your timetable – when your classes are, when study groups are meeting and so on.

On a calendar, mark which assessments are due, examinations are taking place, any field trips and so on.

2. Sorting Out Your Week

Here comes the fun bit... But, it does make me think of Rimmer from *Red Dwarf*. If you aren't familiar, Rimmer is a fictional character who procrastinates by creating a timetable for his studies. He spends so much time creating it, color-coding it and making it look nice that there is no time left to study!

You're going to do a simple and quick version of Rimmer's masterpiece.

Simply draw up your week so it fits onto a page – I prefer days along the top, and times down the side (in hourly lots). For the rest of it, I suggest using one color for each area of your life.

Now, write in your classes, study groups, work and any other fixed commitments. Don't forget to include travel time.

Next, fill in a daily activity for you – so, bring out your list from step 4 above and write in what you feel is humanly manageable.

Then, fill in study time – research, reading, and writing... I recommend blocking time in for each subject. Break this up so that every 90 minutes, you take 15 minutes to shift your focus. This could be

enjoying a cup of tea, walking around the block or meditating. These mini-breaks will refresh, reenergize and refocus you. It is amazing how much more productive you can be when you schedule and take these breaks.

Fill in chores – they still need to get done. Things like cleaning, cooking, doing the groceries... Make sure you plan time to prepare your good food. I used to

use Sunday afternoons for this – I would cook for the week and make good use of the freezer, freezing meals in portion sizes.

Reflect back on your plan. Is it overfilled? Have you got space to catch up if you need to? To rest? To have fun? If not, revise it so that you do. If so, well done!

1. Rewards

This is the most important step. This is the one that will help you get through with a smile.

Like in Step 5, where we talked about the ultimate goal, this step provides you with mini-goals.

At the start of every week, schedule in something that is just for fun. This is your reward for the week. It can be used to push you through those times where you just don't want to do any study... For example, "I can go to the comedy club on Thursday if I get my work done."

You can have daily rewards to, such as, having dinner with friends if the whole day's work is completed in time.

Remember that you can do anything in life, as long as you dearly want to. Shine and Succeed.

~~~

Thank you to my host, Gina Akao.

Challenge Contains Change

I always seem to describe life as a journey. I know that is not a unique viewpoint, but it really seems to sum up a lot of what it is about.

Some people seem to cruise through life, whilst those on the other end of the spectrum seem to be fraught with difficulties, and the rest are somewhere in between. Despite the outward appearances, I don't think for any of us that life is totally smooth all of the time.

There are hurdles, difficulties, and decisions to be made. These may be easy, painful or confusing. Everyone has suffered at some stage, and it is what we do with this suffering that makes the point of difference.

Ultimately it comes down to reacting and responding.

In every instance, there is a chance for us to make a choice. The moment may be incredibly brief – to the point that it is virtually imperceptible, however, it is there. Other times it will be much more obvious.

There will be times when it feels like you are on a ship in rough seas. Where everything slides this way, then that. The movement of the boat is strong, it makes you feel sick and you become disoriented. Another wave crashes over the boat, drenching you from head to toe as you slip and slide to another edge. What do you do? How do you move forwards? Where *is* forwards?

When you are groping your way around the boat, being sloshed all about and not knowing which way is up and which way is down, it is nigh on impossible to make good decisions.

So what do you do?

You find a spot. You hold your ground. You observe.

You begin to see the situation more clearly. You get an insight into the bigger picture. As you get this clarity, you begin to calm down, to see things for what they are and you start to see a way forward.

When the time is right, with this clarity, you can move towards your light – towards everything you are here to do, the life you deserve and the person you are meant to be.

But the clarity from the situation can only be attained from stepping out of it, reorienting yourself and becoming calm inside.

This is when you *respond* to the situation.

Life can throw some real fireballs at us – sometimes they have hidden thorns, too. But life is really only throwing challenges to enable us to change.

Change is hard, but challenges are the opportunities for us to dig deep, reach into the depths of our being and turn the situation into a positive.

This is a true moment of alchemy.

You are creating a magical transformation when you regain your bearings, dig deep and turn the situation into a positive. Where there are struggles and challenges, there are opportunities for growth.

Life's journey is about developing as a person, growing into our soul purpose and doing what we are here to do.

If you get caught up in the drama of every situation, every challenge, every incident, you can't grow because you are so busy reacting.

Reacting is the knee-jerk behavior. Let me illustrate this.

A small child licks an ice cream, enjoying the coolness, the colors and the taste of this delicious treat, when SPLAT! The ice cream lands on the hot ground.

The child who reacts is the one who screams and cries.

The child who responds is the one who is fascinated by their treat changing form, by the colors merging together and creating new ones, by the way the ice cream now runs along the ground following the slope and the cracks in the pavement.

So when you are faced with a challenge, do you scream back at it? Or do you consider it, and find the golden lining?

What is your current tendency?

By recognizing it, you are able to change it. Awareness is the first step, but I am sure you already know that.

I am a fan of playing with words, hence the title of this piece... Take the word "change" and add an "lle" into the middle of it. See? It makes "challenge." So here is the action that I would like you to take: whenever you are in a challenging situation, take the 'ell out of it and see it as a heavenly opportunity for you to create change.

Shine and Succeed!

~~~

© 2014 Lucinda Curran

Thank you to my host Dr Gail Siler.

Blog Posts

What follows are some articles from Lucinda Curran's blog, which can be read at

www.EcoHealthSolutions.com.au/blog

When You've Got A Goal – What Matters?

When you have your eyes set on your target, what matters?

Is it only the end result, is it your journey there, or is it both?

What I want to explore is the signposts to you achieving your goal.

What Will Be Your Measures Of Success?

When we set goals, we know what we want. If we set a measurable goal, we have indicators to let us know that we have reached them.

Often we set audacious goals for ourselves that take time and effort to achieve them.

Along the way we need signposts letting us know we are on track and heading in the right direction.

So how do you determine these?

Product or Process – Which Will It Be?

Years ago, when I was studying to become an early childhood teacher, our Visual Arts teacher would often talk about product versus process.

What she meant was how did the end-result artwork look as opposed to what the child went through when they created it?

Imagine, if you will, some deliciously soft finger paint. Imagine squelching some between your fingers, delighting in the sensation and then marveling at the way you could use it to make mark on the table... That when you dragged your finger through it, you could make pictures within the paint... then getting hold of a different colour, watching them mix together – the swirls of colour, how the red and the yellow came together to make orange. Then, adding blue... the contrast. The fascination as the orange changed... got darker and formed a brown. When you were finished, the teacher came and took a print from it so you could take it home.

Well, the print is of a brown splat. It really doesn't look that nice, but the feeling <u>you</u> get when you look at it is pride and delight – it was SO wonderful to make it.

The process is the delightful journey, the product is the brown splat transferred onto the paper.

So, with your signposts, are you looking for product or process?

Adding Some Inspiration

The inspiration for me to write this came from the conversation I had with a client of mine who is working on achieving better health and a more ideal weight.

Her focus is on the process. By that, she isn't obsessing about calories and meal-times.

Her focus is on putting healthy behaviours in place for her long-term wellbeing. She knows that these will help her to lose weight, but that is not her emphasis.

This has given her enormous freedom on this journey.

She doesn't need to step onto the scales with baited breath, she isn't going to crumble because the scales went the wrong way, she isn't "throwing the towel in" because she did make an unhealthy choice here and there.

She is wholeheartedly focused on the fact that she is changing old entrenched habits and replacing them with ones that will put her in good stead for the rest of her life.

When she makes an unhealthy choice, that hasn't ruined the day – it is serving as a reminder as to WHY she is on the path that she has chosen.

By focusing on the process, she can celebrate the moments where she resisted the urge to eat something not so good, when she decided to take some time for herself, when she feels refreshed each day because she ate well the day before.

By focusing on the process, you can celebrate the gains – as this is where your focus is.

How Are You Going To Set Your Signposts?

Take inspiration from this wonderful woman.

Shift your focus to the journey – the process.

See the positives, learn from the negatives, and blossom.

Celebrate when you reach a landmark – celebrate in a way that propels you towards your goal.

Find the joy in each new step you take.

your notes

On Procrastination: A Great Insight That I Left Out Of My Book

In *Conversations About The Self: Exploring Ideas From Change Your Life Radio*, I explore the concept of procrastination.

My research uncovered it is a bit of a "testy" topic and that many people see it as negative and to be avoided. Whereas, I have found that it can be really useful, part of the creative process and supportive of productivity.

Another Face Of Procrastination

One aspect I did not discuss was the one where you avoid doing something because you know the next task is undesirable.

To illustrate, here's a story about Jackie.

> When Jackie was a teenager, she had a part-time job as a cashier, at the time referred to as a checkout chick. Her part-time job gave her a small disposable income that helped her along while she was still at school. Let's face it this is not the most exciting job to have. But, it was a job – and an easy one.
>
> Anyway, Jackie loved to go out to see live music. She thrived on the energy of the music and it really gave her a "buzz" for a week or so afterwards.
>
> One Friday she was out seeing one of her favourite bands. The time was ticking away and she knew she had to be at work for a 9am start. Midnight came and went, Jackie looked at her watch and declared, "If I don't go home, I don't have to go to bed. If I don't go to bed, I won't have to get up to go to work."
>
> And that is what she did.
>
> She managed to duck home for long enough to have a shower and get changed. And appeared at work – and was alright. Not as bright and chatty as usual, but she did it.
>
> Having achieved it once, she did it a few more times.

Teenage years are great, even your twenties, because you can get away with this... for a while.

Eventually, Jackie had to admit the obvious. Whether she went to bed or not, she still had to go to work.

So, my question for you is: **Have you ever done this?**

Is there something looming that you just don't want to do? Do you do whatever you can to avoid it?

This is all a form of procrastination – and it is not one of the helpful types.

In Jackie's case, she still had to go to work – but she was putting unnecessary pressure on herself.

So, I want you to have a think about it. Is there something (it could be a one-off event or a recurring one) that you try to avoid?

Write down whatever comes up for you.

Now, think about it realistically – and honestly.

If you avoid the preceding tasks, does it make the big-bad-scary one go away? If not, then you need to rethink your strategy.

- What can you do to ease yourself into the big-bad-scary?
- What preparation can you do?
- Is there some sort of support that you need to reach out for to make the big-bad-scariness of it shrink away?

What is the button that you can push to minimise it?

Once, my brother Steven suggested to me a way of shrinking things.

He reminded me of the television that had as children, and that when we turned it off the screen would shrink to a dot and then vanish.

That is something you can do to the big-bad-scary tasks ahead.

The task may remain, but the attached fears, concerns and stress can vanish.

It all starts with being honest with yourself in recognising what is going on. Then you can figure out why? And, what to do?

The main thing to identify here is what procrastination strategy you are using. This is key so that you can easily and quickly recognise it in the future, and take action to halt the procrastination, and get you into a place of healthy action-taking.

Feel empowered – you can change not only the lead-up and the outcome, but also how you handle the situation by being honest with yourself, aware and taking action.

Shine and succeed!

your notes

What My Mum Got Right

Too often I hear people blaming all that is wrong in their lives on their parents.

I guess it's a big part of our culture, and I think it is based in Freud's thinking. I am not talking James Freud, although he was one clever bunny. But I am talking Sigmund.

Sigmund related much of our adult behaviours and problems to what happened in childhood. Maybe we had problems toilet-training, so that makes us "anally retentive," or trouble with being weaned from the breast – and, no, fellas, that does not excuse any breast obsessions!

Parents are human. Parents became parents without training, without manuals, without rule books. They had to work it out as they went. None are perfect. The absolute majority did what they thought was best at the time.

I want to dedicated this blog to my mother who is now in her eighties.

Mum brought us up on her own (at least for the first six years of my life). She somehow managed to make ends meet on the tiny pension she got, with both of us below school-age. How she managed this, I don't think I will ever know, this is not what I want to share with you today.

What I want to share are some of her ingenious child-rearing practices.

- **Calendar Days** (this only works if there are two children)

Calendar Days is a system by which children get equal turns at things. My brother chose to be even, and I chose odd (funny that!). Every second day, you got to choose which shows to watch on television, which records (aka CDs) we would listen to, and even which bedtime story was to be shared. Any choice that needed to be made was made by the one who's "day it was." Genius!!

- **The Fine System**

We got given a small amount of "pocket money" – I think it was $1 a week. Pocket Money day was the same day each week. There were no advances. It was how it was.

Linked in with this, was a Fine System. All of our unacceptable behaviour was given a monetary value, and it would come off our pocket money.

If following the rules was really hard one week, you may not end up with much, or sometimes none at all.

We quickly learned that there were consequences for our actions. Consequences that we didn't like.

At a later stage, a Reward System was also introduced. This meant that is we did above and beyond our usual jobs we would get a set reward.

- **The Ejector Seat Button**

This one was scary!

My brother and I liked to bicker in the car – well, to be honest, I think we bickered anywhere and everywhere. Poor Mum had to somehow drive AND cope with us.

Hence the invention of the Ejector Seat Button.

Even whilst writing this I say it with awe and fear.

In the midst us carrying on, Mum would calmly state, "I am reaching for the Ejector Seat Button," as she leaned slightly towards the gear stick.

Both of us had fertile imaginations, the vision of us flying out through the roof of the car and up into the air was vivid!

It worked every single time! (Hey, it might even still work now!)

- **The Bedtime Story**

Often at the end of the day, Mum was exhausted. She was too tired to read. But she also highly valued the bedtime story (I think no child should ever go to sleep without a bedtime story, but I digress).

So, she would lay back on the bed and tell us one.

Vivid imaginations certainly ran in the family – and I am very grateful that they do!

- **Belief in Us**

Mum has been amazing.

She has been such a great mother, and also such a great friend.

This final thing I am about to share with you is one of the most incredible things that my mother has ever done. She does it day in, day out. She does not falter in it. She does not even realise the power of what she has done. She only knows about it because I thank her again and again.

She believes in us.

She is honest. She will tell us what she really thinks. She expresses her concerns. She may even advise against. But, whatever it is that we choose to do, she supports us no matter what.

She honestly, and completely, believes in us.

I think that this is the most valuable gift a parent can give.

It means that we believe in ourselves, too.

I appreciate the efforts of my amazing mother, and have found her a great inspiration throughout my life.

I hope that these five ideas of hers will be a massive inspiration to you, too!

your notes

Why Are All Men Such B*****ds?

Annie sits across from me in our favourite cafe, sobbing. She's just broken up with Mr Fabulous – this one lasted six weeks. She is heart-broken.

So many questions: "Why? Why? How?" and worse still, "What's wrong with me?"

Annie's latest Mr Fabulous (Mr F) was almost identical to all the other Mr F's she's ever been out with, entangled with, or been attracted to. They are all the same.

You know how this story goes. You've been there too, or you know someone else who has.

And every time it ends, she is devasted and JUST KNOWS it's something to do with her.

Well, it isn't, and yet, it is.

The reason why these relationships end is because they are not right for her. It's a bad match. Clear to an observer, but devastingly unclear to Annie.

How is it her then?

Well, I'm not saying that she is deeply flawed. What I am saying is that she is making the same choice. She is looking in the same places.

"Why are all men such b*****ds?" she will lament in, hmm, about another week or so from now.

Are they? I don't think they are.

The men she chooses are, and she chooses the same types of people over and over again. It doesn't work now, it didn't back then. But she just keeps choosing them.

If you search and look under every rock, you will find the type of guy that dwells under rocks. My cynical friends might call them "snakes." If you search in muddy swamps, no doubt you will find the rhinos or pigs. Just like searching in pubs leads you to... well, you know what I mean.

If this is what you want, go for it.

But if what you want is something different, then you need to look somewhere else. The guys that bring a ray of sunshine into the room aren't going to be in the back corner of a dark gloomy cave. They will be up high, shining brightly, so try looking up instead.

Hold the horses, really, before we look out there, let's look inside.

Usually, there is a lot to heal. I always recommend that between relationships, people need at least a year to heal. Not just to rediscover who you were (women are incredibly good at losing themselves in relationships) but to discover who you are now.

Sounds pretty much the same, but it's not.

I'm talking some serious soul-searching, deep-digging, demon-facing time.

When we repeatedly make the same choices, especially ones that end badly, we are not "getting" the lessons from our experiences.

Why not? Maybe because we are not ready to learn or change.

How do we get these lessons? People are different, so different things work for different people.

One technique I really like is to make lists. Lists mean I can clear my head. Lists mean I can see what I am thinking/feeling... Lists mean I can make comparisons.

Try making a list (or a table) of all the ex's. Write down the things you liked about them and the things you didn't. Be honest. This is just for you.

Find the common elements – positive and negative.

Try to see the pattern – because there IS one.

See if you can make the link back to you – why are you always choosing the same thing? This can be a painful process, and sometimes it is worth coming back to in a few days time. Sometimes it is best to do it with the help of a professional (eg a clinical psychologist).

Then, make a new list. This list ideally should be pages long. Make a list of all the attributes you would like in a partner. Not just any partner, your ideal partner.

Honestly reflect on this list. Is there any reason that you are not pursuing this? Anything that is holding you back here will mean that Mr Perfect cannot be a part of your life. These reasons will need to be sorted out properly.

Sometimes the reasons may be "I'm not ready for a 'real' relationship,"or "I don't deserve this," or "I'm not good enough"...

Well, sister (or brother), let me tell you here and now – YOU DESERVE THE VERY BEST. We all do. We also "owe" the world something – we need to be the very best person that we can be.

Constantly strive to do your very best and be your best. Remember that this does not mean you have to be perfect at all times – gee, we're human, that's not possible. But, as long as we are doing our best, we cannot possibly regret and lament that we should have done/been better.

your notes

How Can I Use My Laptop or Device Safely? 3 Tips To Reduce Your EMR Exposure

With my work as a Building Biologist, I often get a range of enquiries from people about different things. One of the biggest areas of questioning is about reducing exposure to electro-magnetic radiation (EMR). The most asked question is, "How can I use my laptop or device safely?"

There are three types of EMR exposure associated with laptops and devices: AC electric fields, AC magnetic fields and high frequency electromagnetic radiation.

Let's cover a bit of the scientific background so it makes more sense.

AC Electric Fields – ELF

The electric fields emitted from many household appliances fall into the category of Extra Low Frequency (ELF). Electric fields are created where there electricity under pressure – which means that any wiring connected to a power source, can emit an electric field.

Further, a buildings' wiring can have an electric field even when there are no appliances plugged in. It is for this reason that I always recommend people to unplug cords from power points when they are not in use.

Electric fields are also proportional to voltage and they decrease with distance from the source. Therefore, keeping away from appliances that are plugged in can reduce exposure.

Common sources include power lines, household wiring, lighting, mobile phone chargers, hair dryers, hair straighteners, irons, kettles, electric blankets, electric ovens, electric hot water systems, electric slab heating, and so on.

ELF electric fields have been associated with Electrical Hypersensitivity Syndrome (EHS), also known as Electrical Sensitivity (ES). This condition can manifest with some or all of these and other symptoms: skin symptoms (a feeling of itchiness or biting, redness, a burning sensation), eye symptoms (redness, dryness, pain), poor concentration, and dizziness. Some other health effects that have been associated with ELF electric fields include sleep disturbances, fatigue, headache, ringing in the ears (tinnitus), and a constant feeling of a cold or flu about to start but not eventuating.

AC Magnetic Fields – ELF

Although magnetic fields exist in nature, such as when the field of the earth causes the compass needle to point to north, it is with man-made magnetic fields that we are mostly concerned.

Magnetic fields are created when an appliance is switched on. That is, it directly relates to a current being drawn.

Magnetic fields arise from the motion of the electrical charge (WHO, 2012) and this is especially the case in alternating current (AC) as the electricity changes direction frequently.

Common sources of ELF magnetic fields include power lines, household wiring, electric blankets, ovens, fridges, waterbeds, lighting, alarm clocks, mobile phone chargers, electric heating, electric hot water systems, and so on.

There is a large body of evidence that links ELF magnetic fields with biological changes. Possible health effects include a reduction in the immune system, abnormal foetal development, changes to cell growth and development, changes or interruptions to the brain and central nervous system (Professor Adey). Other linked or suspected health effects include breast cancer, miscarriage, depression and suicide.

High Frequency Electromagnetic Radiation – HF

On the electromagnetic spectrum, high frequency (HF) is between 3kHz and 300GHz. At this level, as the two cannot be separated, we measure the combined electric and magnetic fields and refer to this as electromagnetic radiation.

There is an ever-increasing range of sources for high frequency electromagnetic radiation as our society moves towards wireless technology – "getting rid of unsightly wires" and adding many layers of convenience to our lifestyles.

Sources include mobile phone towers, DECT cordless telephones, satellite transmitters, mobile phones, tablets and i-pads, wireless games such as Wii and X-Box, many baby monitors, wireless computer accessories including printer, keyboard, and mouse, wireless internet connections, smart meters and so on.

Numerous health concerns have been linked with HF electromagnetic radiation. These include disturbed sleep, headaches, learning difficulties, concentration problems, fatigue, waking feeling unrefreshed, anxiety, depression, muscle and joint aches and pains, ringing in the ears, hearing loss, palpitations, and more. As well, there have been some links made to brain tumours, epilepsy, blood pressure, and lowered immunity.

How Can I Use My Laptop or Device Safely?

3. Laptops and devices have a massive advantage over the desktop computer, in the eyes of a Building Biologist.

This advantage is that they can be used on battery. Anything that is plugged in uses AC power. AC stands for "alternating current." Alternating current is where electricity passes back and forth through the wires. In contrast, a battery uses DC, or "direct current" – which only goes one way. In short, DC is safer than AC.

Unplug the charger and use your laptop or device on battery.

2. No matter what, I always recommend that you used wired connections – for Internet, mouse and keyboard.

This point is a bit of a 3-for-1 deal – I can't just give you three tips!

Ultimately, this tip is about reducing your exposure to the high frequency end of the electromagnetic spectrum – the one that is about to move up to 4G and 5G!

Here's the best things that you can do – get a keyboard and mouse that you can plug into your laptop. (Devices don't have this option, so I would suggest using a stylus instead of your fingers.)

Using the wired keyboard and mouse means that you have a greater distance from your laptop, which is always a good thing. It also means that you are not relying on a wireless (high frequency connection).

Using a wired Internet connection is part of this solution. However, you will also need to turn off the Wi-Fi capabilities on your computer or it will constantly be searching for a connection (and thus defeating the purpose of using a wired connection) AND you will need to have a modem that does not have Wi-Fi capabilities.

Finding one can be a little tricky. I located some at my local office supply store. I got a modem that had no aerial and only worked via Ethernet connections. It only cost about $50.

So, swap your wireless bits and pieces for wired/cabled equivalents.

1. Despite its name, do not EVER use your laptop (or device) on your lap.

We have already discussed the health implications above, and I have pointed out that distance is the key. But, the other thing to think about is that by having it on your lap, it is close to your reproductive organs.

Science is only beginning to recognise and accept that there can be health effects beyond the thermal changes. As a bit of background information, when radar began to be used mid last century, the thermal effects of radiofrequencies were recognised as problematic for health. The thermal effects on the body have been used as the measuring stick for health effects, despite the fact that there are a vast array of health effects, some of which I have mentioned above, that have nothing to do with your tissues being warmed.

Therefore, never use your laptop or device when it is in contact with your body.

There you have it – 3 tips to help you use your laptop or device more safely.

I hope you have found this information helpful. Please feel free to get in touch with me if there is more you would like to hear about.

About The Publisher: Building Vitality

Building Vitality's aim is to search out books that:

- Offer a unique approach to health and vitality;

- Books that empower the reader with skills and knowledge, which in turn can be used by the reader to enrich their lives; and

- Books that build vitality.

Our motto is "Knowledge is power – so empower yourself today."

We are the "new kids" and it is our mission to bring you the very best books around ~ ones that support you in building vitality into every aspect of your life.

Done-For-You Services

We also offer Done-For-You Services for authors and small businesses. Our services include video trailers, branding, book covers, bookmarks, website graphics and more.

Keep an eye on what we are up to by visiting us at www.BuildingVitality.com.au

your notes

your notes